FAITH

Faith
A Guide to Following God

Henry Dieterich

SERVANT BOOKS
Ann Arbor, Michigan

Published by Servant Books
P.O. Box 8617
Ann Arbor, Michigan 48107

Cover design by Charles Piccirilli and Robert Coe
Cover photo by Four By Five, Inc.

88 89 90 91 92   10 9 8 7 6 5 4 3 2 1

Printed in the United States of America
ISBN 0-89283-356-4

Library of Congress Cataloging-in-Publication Data

Dieterich, Henry.
    Faith: a guide to following God / Henry Dieterich.
        p.   cm.—(The Catholic Bible study guide series)
    "Based on the teachings of Ralph Martin"—p.
    ISBN 0-89283-356-4
    1. Faith—Biblical teaching. 2. Bible—Study. I. Martin,
Ralph, 1942—   .II. Title. II. Series.
BS680.F27D54   1988   88-28186
234'.2'076—dc19   CIP

Contents

Acknowledgment

The authors of the *Catholic Bible Study Guides* wish to acknowledge the invaluable contribution made by Nick Cavnar in developing the format for individual study used in these guides.

Introduction

Faith is the basis of Christianity. Faith is our first approach to God and the foundation for any relationship with him. If we do not first believe, then nothing else in Christian life or teaching makes sense.

Faith is both a gift of God and a virtue to be cultivated, something we can grow in. It is something we come to by turning our lives over to God. It refers both to our belief in certain truths and our trust in the living God.

This guide is intended as an introduction to what the Bible says about faith: what it is, how it affects our life, and how to have more of it. It is not an exhaustive treatment of the question; there are many theological issues it does not even begin to cover. One could find a whole library of books on the subject and spend a lifetime reading them. The passages of Scripture discussed in this guide are only a few of those that talk about faith. This study of faith only introduces a few of the questions and provides some basis for beginning a life of faith or growing in faith.

This guide has another purpose: not only to teach *about* faith, but also to help you to have faith and to increase the faith you already have. Like Scripture itself, it is intended not only to be informative, but also to be effective and practical. My prayer is that as you read it, your own faith will grow and deepen.

How to Use This Guide

There are many ways to study the Bible. Scholars acquire expertise in the original biblical languages and often other related ones as well. They immerse themselves in history, commentaries, and other studies, all in an effort to help us understand the meaning of the inspired authors. Their contribution is very valuable. In fact, if you have a popular commentary it probably includes some of the fruit of their labor. But this is not a study of this kind. You do not need to know Greek or Hebrew, nor do you need any specialized training. This study simply looks at the Bible as God's Word and seeks to discover the simple meaning of the text.

All you need to use this book is a Bible and a heart and mind open to God's wisdom. I have provided space in the guide for you to write down answers to questions and to fill out charts and exercises. It would help to keep a notebook as well to write down other observations and reflections you might have. If you have a simple commentary that you already know how to use, that might help you to understand the passages referred to, but it is not required.

Each of the nine studies should take at least an hour. Set aside the time so that you can work without interruptions. Begin by asking God to open your heart to his Word, then proceed in a spirit of prayer. Pause occasionally to pray and reflect on what you have been learning.

The nine individual, hour-long studies in each guide are divided into three parts that build steadily in your understanding of faith. For example, the first part explores what faith is, why it's important, and how we receive it. On the other hand, the last part of the study guide considers some important helps in living a life of faith: prayer, Scripture, and the Eucharist. You'll find each individual study will explore some facet of faith by focusing on one or more key Scripture passages. To help direct your time, I have opened each study with a brief commentary.

However, the heart of the studies are the questions and exercises where you investigate the Scriptures in depth with a focus on some aspect of faith. It is important that you look up and read carefully each passage referred to, including secondary Scripture references. God's Word is a unity, and each part helps us understand the whole wisdom of God.

Each of the nine lessons also contains a tip for growing in faith. This is a way of applying the message of the commentary and your study of Scripture to everyday life. Read these tips over carefully and try to use them. Perhaps you could make a resolution to concentrate on putting one into practice each week as you go through the guide. They will help you to make faith more of a reality in your life.

At the end of each study, there is an optional memory verse. If you memorize this verse, you will have in your mind a brief summary of the study you've just completed. Since the early church, Christians have found that memorizing and "chewing on" God's Word has helped build up their faith.

The most important aid to doing this study, however, is the Holy Spirit. He is the one who inspired the written Scriptures in the first place. Ask for his help as you go through this book.

Bring Others to Faith in Christ

One way to use this guide is to introduce others to faith in Jesus Christ as Lord. The individual studies are designed so that they can serve as an introduction to basic Christian truth, even for those who know very little about Christianity. If you know someone—maybe a neighbor, co-worker, friend, or family member—who needs such an introduction, decide either to review or go through the material with that person. If you yourself are new to the Christian message, find a mature Christian you trust and see if you can discuss the individual studies with him or her as you work your way through the guide. No book or guide can ever substitute for personal contact in sharing the Word of God.

Questions for Group Discussion

With this important point about personal contact in mind, I have included five questions for group discussion at the end of each study. If possible, I do recommend that you go through the study guide with a group from your local parish, prayer group, or community. You will benefit from the insight and practical help offered by others in your group.

You could also organize an evangelistic Bible study group in your neighborhood or at work. If you are interested in taking this approach, I suggest that you organize the group with two or three other Christians who are willing to commit themselves to such an evangelistic Bible study. That way you will have the support of other committed Christians in introducing your neighbors, friends, or co-workers to faith in Jesus Christ as Lord.

Group members will need to commit themselves to finishing each study on faith before meeting as a group. Also, you'll want to develop a format, an approach to leadership, and a set time for your group meeting. I suggest that you open and close each group discussion with a short time of prayer. It might be helpful as well to have someone read the main Scripture passage for study before you begin your discussion. That way the passage for study will be fresh in everyone's mind. After the formal close of your group meetings, you may want to have some time for informal fellowship. This will give group members an opportunity to get to know each other better in a more relaxed atmosphere.

Keep in mind that the questions for discussion should be used flexibly, depending on the needs of your group. If you spend a full discussion session on one question, that's fine. Depending on the nature of the group, you may also want to develop some of your own questions for discussion.

My prayer is that as you use this guide, you may come to a deeper faith in God and a greater understanding of his Word in holy Scripture.

Part I:

The Importance of Faith, What It Is, and How We Receive It

To grow in faith, we first need to understand why it's important, what it is, and how we go about receiving it. That's why our first three studies will lay a foundation by covering these three important areas. Once that foundation has been laid we can then turn to Parts II and III which discuss our critical need for faith, God's answer in Jesus Christ, and some of the important means God has given us to grow in faith.

Study 1—Matthew 17:14-20
The Importance of Faith

When they came to the crowd a man approached, knelt down before him, and said, "Lord, have pity on my son, for he is a lunatic and suffers severely; often he falls into fire, and often into water. I have brought him to your disciples, but they could not cure him." Jesus said in reply, "O faithless and perverse generation, how long will I be with you? How long will I endure you? Bring him here to me." Jesus rebuked him and the demon came out of him, and from that hour the boy was cured. Then the disciples approached Jesus in private and said, "Why could we not drive it out?" He said to them, "Because of your little faith. Amen, I say to you, if you have faith the size of a mustard seed, you will say to this mountain, 'Move from here to there,' and it will move. Nothing will be impossible for you." (Mt 17:14-20)

Here is a situation that many of us today can understand. The man in this story came to Jesus with a very contemporary problem. His son had a mental disorder that led him to do self-destructive things. The disorder was caused by a demon in this case. Even Jesus' disciples could do nothing about it.

But Jesus could. He cured the boy by casting out the demon. Yet he didn't leave it at that. When the disciples asked him why they had not been able to do it, he didn't answer, "Because I'm the Son of God and you're not." Rather he told them that they could do it if they only had one thing: faith. Faith, even a tiny bit of faith, would make it possible to shift a whole mountain, Jesus told them.

What a wonderful thing faith must be if it can do that! This isn't the only place where Jesus promises that faith can do great things. Over and over again, he speaks of "believing" and ascribes miraculous powers to faith.

In Mark 11:22-24, Jesus again promises that faith can move mountains—not just from place to place this time but actually into the sea! He adds, "All that you ask in prayer, believe that you will receive it and it shall be yours" (v. 24). In Luke 9:23, in another version of the story of the lunatic boy we have just read, Jesus says, "Everything is possible to one who has faith."

One of the practical effects of faith is healing, or as Jesus presents it many times in the Gospels, being saved from illness. When a woman who had suffered many years from an incurable hemorrhage merely touched the hem of Jesus' garment, she was healed. Among all the people who were crowding around him, he perceived that someone had touched him in a special way. When she approached him, he told her what had made the difference. "He said to her, 'Daughter, your faith has saved you. Go in peace and be cured of your affliction'" (Mk 5:34).

This woman is not the only person in the Gospels who is saved and healed by faith. Bartimaeus, a blind man who lived in Jericho, cried out to Jesus for his sight and received it. It was his faith that made this possible. "Jesus told him, 'Go your way; your faith has saved you'" (Mk 10:52). Two other blind men received the same favor, as Jesus says to them, "Let it be done for you according to your faith" (Mt 9:29).

Jesus in fact urges, even commands, those who hear him to have faith. To a synagogue official whose daughter has just died, he says, "Just have faith and she will be saved" (Lk 8:50). On the other hand, he criticizes those who do not have faith. Matthew 8:23-27 tells the story of Jesus and his disciples during a storm at sea. This is a time when anyone would be terrified, as the disciples were. But before Jesus calms the storm, he criticizes them for being afraid: "Why are you terrified, O you of little faith?" he says (Mt 8:26). Even in the most difficult circumstances, he is saying that we still ought to have faith.

Everywhere we look in the Gospels, we see faith spoken of. Jesus commends those who have faith and criticizes those who do not, or those who do not have enough. When he speaks to "doubting Thomas," he says, "Do not be unbelieving, but believe" (Jn 20:27). The faith spoken of here is not just an idea, but has practical implications. We can receive anything we want through faith. People are healed by faith of incurable diseases and blindness. And Jesus tells us that if we have faith, we can even move mountains.

In fairy tales, we often read about magic rings or lamps that grant wishes to their owners. When we read such stories, we think, "Wouldn't it be great to have a thing like that?" As we grow up, we learn that such things don't exist. We get cynical. We decide to "tough it out."

While faith certainly isn't a magic ring or a lamp that will automatically grant our every wish, it does point to unseen realities that hold out the hope of reward to those who seek God. The question then becomes: What if there is a way that the fundamental problem of life itself can be addressed by faith in God? What if God has provided a way that will satisfy our restless hearts? Wouldn't that be well worth having? Wouldn't that be a treasure far exceeding anything we can imagine or hope for?

Study: Matthew 17:14-20.

1. Read verses 14-16.
This account is also told by Mark (Mk 9:14-29) and by Luke (9:37-43). Scan these two other versions of this incident. In Mark's version notice that the father of the boy says to Jesus, "I do believe, help my unbelief!" How does the father in this particular account show belief? What exactly does he believe in?

(a) _____

_____

(b) _____

_____

How can someone believe and not believe at the same time? Think of some time or situation in your life when you believed and disbelieved at the same time. For instance, many of us as we grow up get cynical about politics. Our earlier idealism gives way to a mixture of belief and disbelief as politicians fail to keep campaign promises we were personally invested in. Intellectually, we may hope the politician we support will carry through on his or her promises, but in our hearts we begin to question it. Take a moment and compare the situation in your own life with that of the father whose son was possessed. Was your response of disbelief appropriate? What about the father's? Why?

(a) _____

_____

(b) _____

_____

(c) _____

_____

2. Read verses 17-18.

This is not the only time in the Gospels that Jesus criticizes someone for a lack of faith. The words in verse 17 occur in the other versions of this event (Mk 9:19; Lk 9:41). Who is Jesus addressing here?

_____

Jesus asks, "How long will I be with you?" What difference would it make whether Jesus were with them or not?

_____

_____

_____

In Matthew 8:26, Mark 4:40, and Luke 8:25, Jesus criticizes his disciples for their lack of faith during a storm at seal. Read one of these accounts of this incident in Scripture. Why should the disciples have had faith in that threatening situation?

_____

_____

_____

What does Jesus do in this case that is similar to what he does in the account of the healing of the boy?

_____

_____

_____

In Matthew 6:30 and Luke 12:28, Jesus refers to his hearers as "O you of little faith." In whom are they supposed to have faith? What are they supposed to expect? Why should they expect it?

(a) _____

(b) _____

(c) _____

Consider one situation in your own life where you have little faith for things to change. What are your expectations? What should you expect?

(a) _____

_____

(b) _____

_____

3. Read verses 19-20.
Jesus speaks of "faith the size of a mustard seed" here and in Luke 17:6. What is there about a mustard seed that is significant here? (Hint: read Mt 13:31-32; Mk 4:30-32; or Lk 13:18-19.)

_____

_____

_____

In Mark 11:22-25, Jesus promises again that faith can move mountains. In whom does he say to have faith? What conditions does Jesus attach to receiving what you ask for?

(a) _____

(b) _____

_____

Summary:

Read over your notes from this study. You should have noted some important characteristics of faith. What are they? What are some good reasons for having faith? What are the results when we do step out in faith?

1. _____

2. _____

_____

3. _____

_____

Tip for Growing in Faith:

You have probably already thought of quite a few problems or situations in your own life where you would like to see the results of faith at work. In thinking about these situations you have probably experienced some anxiety. How can you have faith if you are troubled with anxiety?

In fact, it is not at all uncommon for someone to feel greater anxiety in first attempting to have faith. This problem is made worse by the way people talk about worry in modern society. People say, "I have a lot to worry about," when what they mean is, "I have a lot to do." Someone says, "I was worried about you," intending it as an expression of sincere concern. People speak as if worrying about things or being anxious will actually be of benefit to themselves or others.

It is helpful to remember that anxiety or worry cannot help the situation—only God can. As Jesus said, "Can any of you by worrying add a single moment to your life-span?" (Mt 6:27). Anxiety is a problem, not a solution. There can never be a need for anxiety. While banishing anxiety from your life may be very difficult (and certainly it is not something to worry about!), we can begin by changing the way we talk about it. If we do not speak of anxiety as something necessary or desirable, then we will not cling to it when the time comes to have faith.

As we learn more about what faith is and the reasons for it, we will find more and more weapons for dealing with anxiety.

Optional Memory Verse:

"Therefore I tell you, all that you ask for in prayer, believe that you will receive it and it shall by yours." (Mk 11:24)

For Group Discussion:

1. What is Jesus trying to teach the disciples about faith in Matthew 17:14-20? Discuss.

2. Why is it so important that we have faith in Jesus? Can't he act in spite of our disbelief?

3. Let everyone in the group share briefly about the situation they thought of in their life where they believed and disbelieved at the same time. Have everyone explain whether or not they thought their disbelief was justified.

4. What exactly does Jesus mean by "faith the size of a mustard seed"? What is the implication? Discuss.

5. What are the important characteristics of faith you can identify from your study?

Study 2—Hebrews 11
Understanding What Faith Is

Faith is the realization of what is hoped for and evidence of things not seen. Because of it the ancients were well attested. By faith we understand that the universe was ordered by the word of God, so that what is visible came into being through the invisible. By faith Abel offered to God a sacrifice greater than Cain's. Through this he was attested to be righteous, God bearing witness to his gifts, and through this, though dead, he still speaks. By faith Enoch was taken up so that he should not see death, and "he was found no more because God had taken him." Before he was taken up, he was attested to have pleased God. But without faith it is impossible to please him, for anyone who approaches God must believe that he exists and that he rewards those who seek him. (Heb 11:1-6)

The eleventh chapter of the letter to the Hebrews is a catalog of the heroes of faith from the Old Testament. It begins by explaining what faith is and mentions that faith pleases God.

"Without faith it is impossible to please him," says verse 6. Then we are given a minimal definition of faith: believing that God exists and that he rewards those who seek him. But there is more to faith than this. Verse 1 defines faith as "the realization of what is hoped for and evidence of things not seen." This definition is profound, but perhaps a bit hard to understand. It doesn't seem at first glance to have much to do with believing that God exists. What does the inspired author of Hebrews mean by this definition?

The word here translated "realization" is a Greek philosophical term *hypostasis* that often means the reality of something as opposed to mere appearance. It can also mean a concrete example of some more general reality. The word "evidence" means "a convincing demonstration." These words do not refer to states of mind, but to something objective. Faith is the decision to accept an unseen reality, specifically the reality of God and his promises. If we have faith, we can act on it in obedience to God's will. Indeed, if we don't, then it's a pretty good sign that our so-called faith is really an illusion.

The examples of faith mentioned in this study illustrate this principle. Abraham is a hero of faith by any account. His story is told in the book of Genesis (chapters 12-25). Here we learn that he "put his faith in the Lord, who credited it to him as an act of righteousness." Specifically, he believed that he, who at the time had no children, would have innumerable descendants, because God had promised it. When God told him to sacrifice his son Isaac, who had been born in accordance with this promise, he was willing to do so. This incident is mentioned in Hebrews 11:17-19. We are told that he did this "by faith" because he believed "that God was able to raise even from the dead."

James, in his letter, cites the incident of the sacrifice of Isaac as an example of "works" as opposed to faith. He also speaks of Rahab (Jas 2:25), who welcomed the Israelite spies, in the same way. Hebrews says that she did this "by faith" (11:31). So which is it?

The answer is that faith is more than just an idea. It is "the *realization* of what is hoped for and *evidence* of things not seen." Faith is something concrete. It requires a response, a "realization." Or as James says, "Just as a body without a spirit is dead, so also faith without works is dead." A dead body is still a body, but it isn't good for much. Dead faith isn't good for much either. That's why so many of the accounts of heroes of the faith in Hebrews 11 turn on something someone *did* because of his or her faith; the person acted as if some unseen thing were nevertheless present. That is why Jesus in Mark 11:24 could say, "Believe that you will receive it, and it shall be yours."

Jesus' promise in Mark gives us an important key to understanding how faith works. Intellectual understanding, although important, isn't enough. We need to believe the revelation of God we have already received through Scripture and tradition, and then act on it. Faith is a way of life that treats what is hoped for as real, that provides evidence for the unseen. If God's existence and his ability to provide for us are just something "in our head," they don't have much power. But if we can put them into practice, then God and his power are really a part of our life.

Study: Hebrews 11.

1. There is no better way to learn what faith means in practice than to look at the great men and women of faith in the Old Testament. Hebrews 11 lists or alludes to a great many of these. Some of them had faith in God for something they had not yet seen and lived to see the fulfillment of their faith. For each of the following, look up the Scripture passages given. Then answer these two questions by filling out the chart below: What unseen reality did this person decide to believe in? What did each one do to put this faith into practice?

Men and Women of Faith	Believed in	Action
Noah (Heb 11:7; Gen 6:11-7:5)		
Abraham (Heb 11:17-19; Jas 2:21; Gn 22:1-18)		
Moses (Heb 11:23-29; Ex 14:15-31)		
Joshua (Heb 11:30; Jos 6:1-21)		
Rahab (Heb 11:31; Jas 2:25; Jos 2:1-21, 6:17-25)		
Gideon (Heb 11:32; Jgs 6-7)		
David (Heb 11:32; 1 Sm 17:32-51)		
The widow of Zarephath (Heb 11:35; 1 Kgs 17:7-24)		
Hezekiah (Heb 11:34; 2 Kgs 18:13-19:36)		

2. A number of others had faith for something they did not live to see. Do the same with these as you did with those in question 1. What did each decide to believe in and why? How did each put his faith into action? How was this hope eventually fulfilled?

Men of Faith	Believed in	Action	Fulfillment
Jacob (Heb 11:21; Gn 48:8-20)			
Joseph (Heb 11:22; Gn 50:24-26)			
Eleazar (Heb 11:35; 2 Mc 6:18-31)			

3. Think of two examples of faith in people that you have known. It might be one of your parents, a grandparent, a parish priest, a nun, or a family friend. How did these two people manifest the faith shown by the great biblical heroes just mentioned?

(a) Person 1: _____

_____

_____

_____

(b) Person 2: _____

_____

_____

_____

How have you grown in practicing your own faith through their example? Explain.

_____

_____

_____

_____

Summary:

Read over your notes from this study. From them you should be able to make some generalizations about men and women of faith. What are the motivations of a person who has faith? What does a person who has faith do?

1. _____

_____

_____

2. _____

_____

_____

Tip for Growing in Faith:

That God exists is not something many people think about much these days. Even if people do not actively disbelieve in God, they do not commonly pay much attention to his existence. The Bible tells us that this is a foolish attitude: "The fool says in his heart, 'There is no God'" (Ps 53:1).

We have seen in this study that having faith begins with believing that God exists. Therefore, if we want to grow in faith, we must not be like the fool. In fact, we must make every action and decision taking God's existence into account. This does not just apply to times when we are praying or doing "spiritual" things. God should be a factor in everything we do. Whenever you make a decision or take any action, remind yourself that God exists. Ask yourself from time to time, "Am I behaving as if God existed? Would I be acting or deciding or thinking differently if he did not exist?"

This may mean doing things differently from those around us. But we should not be afraid of this. Make it a habit to take God into account. If you are afraid that other people might think you a little odd, remember that it is the fool who denies God's existence. You are the one in touch with reality. It is an unseen reality, but it is nevertheless powerful.

Optional Memory Verse:

Faith is the realization of what is hoped for and evidence of things not seen. (Heb 11:1)

For Group Discussion:

1. Discuss the two definitions of faith that are mentioned in the opening commentary. What kind of faith are we called to have as Christians?

2. How are the men and women of God mentioned in Hebrews 11 examples of the Christian definition of faith? What do they believe in and then how do they act on it?

3. How do Jacob, Joseph, and Eleazar continue to have faith for something when they do not live to see the fulfillment of what God promised? What is the key to their perseverance and faithfulness?

4. Give everyone in the group a chance to share about someone who was an inspiring example of faith to them. What made this person a particularly inspiring example of faith?

5. What have you learned about living out your faith from this study? Has your understanding of what faith is changed?

Study 3—Romans 10:5-18
How We Go about Getting Faith

But how can they call on him in whom they have not believed? And how can they believe in him of whom they have not heard? And how can they hear without someone to preach? And how can people preach unless they are sent? As it is written, "How beautiful are the feet of those who bring [the] good news!" But not everyone has heeded the good news; for Isaiah says, "Lord, who has believed what was heard from us?" Thus faith comes from what is heard, and what is heard comes through the word of Christ. (Rom 10:14-17)

"Hey, have you heard the good news?" Our neighbor or co-worker rushes up to us, flashing a big smile. We just can't wait to hear what it is. We've got the day off tomorrow? Everyone's getting a raise? The home team won the championship? Our friend's daughter is engaged? Whatever it is, we're eager to hear, and happy to have learned about it. If we never found out or if we didn't believe it, we couldn't share whatever joy it was. The news, whatever it was, would still be true, but it wouldn't be a part of our life. What we hear about, on the other hand, is something we now know and can act on.

That's how it is with faith in God. We acquire it by hearing a message. That message tells us that God exists, that he is worthy of our trust, and, even more importantly, that he is eager to give us what we need.

This message is what Paul in his letter to the Romans calls "the good news"—or to use an old word that means the same thing, the gospel. When Jesus went around preaching, his message was, "This is the time of fulfillment. The kingdom of God is at hand. Repent, and believe in the gospel" (Mk 1:15).

The gospel, the "good news," is what Paul calls "the word of Christ," that is, the Word *about* Christ: who he is and how he fulfills God's plan for human history. When Jesus preached this gospel, he was in fact proclaiming that his own presence on the earth brought about the "time of fulfillment." The "kingdom of God" to which he continually referred was not a territorial kingdom but a state or period of history when God's reign or authority would be present to the world. Jesus himself brought this authority with him. As he says in Matthew 12:28, "If it is by the Spirit of God that I drive out demons, then the kingdom of God has come upon you."

Those who hear and believe the gospel are those who have faith, because hearing is where faith starts. Jesus could reliably proclaim the power of faith because he himself was the one who could give that power to those who believed in him. He tells his disciples during the Last Supper, "Amen, amen, I say to you, whoever believes in me will do the works that I do, and will do greater ones than these, because I am going to the Father" (Jn 14:12).

When we believe this Word, we agree to the truth of God's unseen plan of salvation, a plan in which Christ has the central role. We take on a new way of looking at the world. Part of this new perspective is the way that God has promised to provide for each one of us what we need and ask.

Believing and entering into this plan is the faith that can move mountains. It is the faith that the great men and women of faith spoken of in Hebrews 11 had. It is the faith that God can give to you and to me when we accept his invitation to "believe the gospel." We can choose one way or the other, since Paul says, "Not everyone has heeded the good news." If you were told there was a special holiday tomorrow, you could ignore the good news and come in to work—but you'd probably have a pretty frustrating time. It's the same with the good news about Christ. You can ignore it and miss out on the benefits of faith if you want to.

Or you can accept it. You can believe the gospel. Then you will not only have access to the benefits of faith, you will also have the key to understanding God's plan for the world and your place in it.

Study: Romans 10:15-18.

1. Read Acts 2:22-41.
This passage depicts the first proclamation of the gospel by the apostles at Pentecost.

(a) What event is at the center of Peter's message?

_____

_____

(b) What does he say this event demonstrates?

_____

_____

(c) What effect does Peter's message have on his audience?

_____

_____

Imagine yourself at the scene. You are hearing this message for the first time. What kind of response do you think you would have?

_____

_____

_____

_____

_____

2. Read Acts 17:22-34.
This passage relates another proclamation of the gospel, this time by Paul, in Athens. How does Paul's presentation differ from Peter's at Pentecost? How is it the same?

(a) The differences: _____

_____

_____

(b) The similarities: _____

_____

_____

What effect does Paul's message have on his audience?

_____

_____

How did the cultural and religious differences between the Athenians and the inhabitants of Jerusalem affect the content of the gospel message and the way people responded:

(a) The content: _____

_____

(b) The response: _____

_____

What does this teach us about presenting the gospel message to others?

_____

_____

_____

3. Read Romans 10:5-18.
Here Paul is discussing the response we need to make to the gospel. What does he say are the stages someone goes through in acquiring faith? List them in order and number them yourself.

_____

_____

_____

_____

_____

_____

How does the preaching of Peter and Paul just mentioned illustrate the steps in this process? Explain.

_____

_____

_____

_____

_____

_____

Imagine that you are about to encounter each of the three people listed below and have an opportunity to share the gospel. How would the content of your message change with each audience? What would remain a constant? Note at least one change and one constant for each audience.

Audience	Changes	Constants
A neighbor who doesn't go to church		
A Chinese immigrant who has never heard the gospel		
A college student doubting the faith		

Summary:

Read over your notes from this study. In simple terms, describe what the gospel is.

_____

_____

_____

_____

_____

Tip for Growing in Faith:

"Faith comes by hearing"—not just at first, but all through the Christian life. One essential aid to growing in faith is having other Christians to encourage us.

In general, it's always a good idea to have other Christians to whom you can give an account of how well you are fulfilling the duties that help you to grow in your relationship with the Lord. One part of this support is reminding you of the presence of God, of his reality, and his promises. It can be a family member, a co-worker, or a good Christian friend. If you want to grow in faith, agree that you will speak words of faith and encouragement to each other whenever it is necessary. Decide to pray for each other. Remember: you will never outgrow your own need to hear the gospel.

Optional Memory Verse:

> *Thus faith comes from what is heard, and what is heard comes through the word of Christ.* (Rom 10:17)

For Group Discussion:

1. Why do Christians consider the gospel message "good news?"

2. Why is it so important that we all hear the gospel message and respond to it at some point in our lives?

3. Compare the preaching of Peter and Paul from your study. What remains the same in both of their preachings? What are the differences? Discuss.

4. Let everyone in the group briefly share about some presentation of the gospel that they found particularly effective. Ask yourselves: what are the elements that made it an effective presentation of the gospel?

5. Are there certain fears you have about sharing your faith with others? How can you overcome them? Discuss.

Part II:

Our Predicament, How Things Got that Way, and God's Answer in Christ Jesus

Now that we know what faith is and how to receive it, we need to realize our predicament—we need to see *why* faith in God is absolutely essential for us. The next three studies will give us a perspective on the state of the world, how it got that way, and then show how God provided a way out for us through the death and resurrection of Jesus.

Study 4—Luke 13:1-5
The State of the World
from the Perspective of Faith

At that time some people who were present there told him about the Galileans whose blood Pilate had mingled with the blood of their sacrifices. He said to them in reply, "Do you think that because these Galileans suffered in this way they were greater sinners than all other Galileans? By no means! But I tell you, if you do not repent, you will all perish as they did! Or those eighteen people who were killed when the tower at Siloam fell on them—do you think that they were more guilty than everyone else who lived in Jerusalem? By no means! But I tell you, if you do not repent, you will all perish as they did!" (Lk 13:1-5)

God sees our problems very differently from the way we do. Faith enables us to to submit our own limited human perspective to God's unlimited eternal perspective. God's perspective is the only undistorted perspective. We need to see as God sees. That is the kind of perspective that Jesus is presenting in this passage.

Disasters were just as much a part of daily life in Jesus' time as they are today. You may have just heard about a flood, an earthquake, a fire, the collapse of a building, or some great injustice somewhere in the world. Our news media are full of them. The Jews of Jesus' time were no different. They lived under the unjust and often cruel Roman government that crushed their nation and despised their religion. This only added to the natural disasters such as the earthquakes to which that part of the world is particularly prone.

Why would such things happen? The Scriptures provided one simple answer, an answer that was in the back of the minds of those people who came to Jesus. Disasters were punishments for sin.

The Old Testament provided many examples of this teaching. In the Book of Deuteronomy, we can read the fullest exposition of the notion that misfortune is punishment for sin. Through Moses, the Lord first promises blessing for following his Law. Then he describes what will happen if the Israelites violate the covenant he has just made with them: "But if you do not hearken to the voice of the LORD, your God, and are not careful to observe all his commandments which I enjoin on you today, all these curses shall come upon you and overwhelm you" (Dt

28:15). He then goes on to list the disasters—famine, diseases, defeat by enemies, exile, and slavery—that would come as punishment for sin against God by violating his law. The Israelites had reason to believe this. Throughout the Exodus, they experienced God punishing them for disobedience, rebellion, and grumbling.

Not only the whole people but individuals are subject to this principle. Disaster, misfortune, and death are the lot of those who sin against God. In the Old Testament, we have numerous examples such as Eli, who allowed his sons to profane the worship of God (1 Sm 2-3), of Saul (1 Sm 15:23), and even of King David, who was "a man after God's own heart." When he sins by taking another man's wife, God forgives his sin, but declares that he will have to face "the sword" within his own house and have his own wives taken by another, a prophecy that was fulfilled by the revolt of his favorite son Absalom. In addition, the son born to the adulterous union will die (2 Sm 12:9-14).

Among the Jewish people, therefore, disaster, whether personal or national, was considered punishment for sin. It was evidence that God takes sin seriously and is not about to let sinners prosper. That is probably why they came to Jesus to ask him about the Galileans. Were these men sinning especially badly? What had they done to deserve this fate? The question was one any rabbi or teacher in Israel would be expected to answer. It is very similar to the one Jesus had to answer in John 9:2: "Who sinned, this man or his parents, that he was born blind?"

What Jesus gives us here is the perspective we should have on all sorts of disasters. Is there an earthquake in Mexico? Are the Mexicans worse sinners than anyone else? Or does it mean that suffering and disaster have nothing to do with God's response to sin? Neither, Jesus tells us. Yes, disasters are warnings from God; but they apply to all of us. "Unless you repent, you will all likewise perish." That is how God looks at it. Things don't "just happen." The eyes of faith can see God operating in all circumstances. And the first thing we see as we look around us, as we watch the evening news, as we read the daily newspaper, is suffering, injustice, and death. How can we understand them? Jesus tells us in this passage what they are: a warning for us to repent.

Study: Luke 13:1-5.

1. Read Numbers 25:1-13.
What sin did the Israelites commit? What was the consequence?

(a) _____

_____

(b) _____

_____

How did Phinehas deal with the problem? What happened to him as a result?

(a) _____

_____

(b) _____

_____

What does this account tell us about God? About his attitude toward sin?

(a) _____

_____

(b) _____

_____

Taking Phinehas as an example, what should be our own attitude about serious sin among God's people?

_____

_____

_____

2. Scan 2 Samuel 12 and 13, especially noting 12:7-25.
God responds to David's sins by punishing him in three ways. What are they? How are each of the punishments appropriate to David's specific sins?

(a) Punishment #1: _____

_____

(b) Punishment #2: _____

_____

(c) Punishment #3: _____

_____

How does David respond to God's judgment? What does he recognize about God's action when he is punished?

(a) _____

_____

(b) _____

_____

Taking David as an example, what should be our reaction when we realize we have sinned and face God's judgment?

_____

_____

_____

3. Read Luke 13:1-5.
(a) What is Jesus saying to his hearers about the state of human beings?

_____

_____

_____

(b) What is he saying about God?

_____

_____

(c) How does Jesus' teaching follow from the lessons we have drawn from our two Old Testament passages?

_____

_____

_____

_____

_____

(d) How is Jesus' teaching different from what we've heard in the Old Testament?

_____

_____

_____

_____

_____

Consider the reaction of those who heard this teaching of Jesus for the first time. How does this teaching give them—and us—new understanding on the state of the world?

_____

_____

_____

_____

_____

Think about a serious sin that is frequently committed in our society today. Consider one that particularly bothers you or even one that has touched you personally in some way. What have been the consequences of this sin in the world at large? List some of them. What do you think your attitude should be toward this sin? Remember: God's punishment for sin is meant to be a warning for *all* of us to repent. If necessary read Luke 13:1-5 again.

(a) _____

_____

_____

(b) _____

_____

_____

Summary:

Read over your notes from this study. What has it taught you about the nature of God? About the nature of sin?

1. _____

_____

_____

2. _____

_____

_____

Tip for Growing in Faith:

One way to help develop God's perspective, not just in observing the world, but in your own life, is to apply it in concrete situations. Our news reports are full of disasters: storms, earthquakes, fires, plane crashes, AIDS—the list is as long as the history of the world.

One normal reaction to hearing about such a disaster would be to think, "I'm glad it wasn't me." Another might be to think that it's because of our own superior goodness that we have escaped. But if you have the perspective that Jesus teaches in Luke 13, the best response is, "It could have been me. In fact, it should have been me. The sins of the whole human race, and especially my sins, deserve the judgment and punishment of God."

Our response to seeing the troubles of the world should not be to pass judgment or to become smug, but to become more humble and repentant ourselves. We should also pray that others will repent and follow Christ wholeheartedly.

Optional Memory Verse:

> *For the wages of sin is death, but the gift of God is eternal life in Christ Jesus our Lord.* (Rom 6:23)

For Group Discussion:

1. How would you characterize the state of the world in Jesus' day? In our day?

2. What does it mean to have a perspective of faith about the state of the world?

3. What should our attitude be about serious sin among God's people? Hint: What is Phinehas' attitude toward the serious sin of the Israelites?

4. In light of God's judgment on sin, what should our response be when we commit sin, especially serious sin? Hint: What is David's reaction when he is confronted with his sin by the prophet Nathan?

5. Share one way you can develop a faith perspective in dealing with problems and sin in your own life. Give everyone in the group an opportunity to share.

Study 5—Genesis 3
How Sin Entered the World

Now the serpent was the most cunning of all the animals that the LORD God had made. The serpent asked the woman, "Did God really tell you not to eat from any of the trees of the garden?" The woman answered the serpent: "We may eat of the fruit of the trees of the garden; it is only about the fruit of the tree in the middle of the garden that God said, 'You shall not eat it or even touch it, lest you die.'" But the serpent said to the woman: "You certainly will not die! No. God knows well that the moment you eat of it your eyes will be opened and you will be like gods who know what is good and what is bad." The woman saw that the tree was good for food, pleasing to the eyes, and desirable for gaining wisdom. So she took some of its fruit and ate it; and she also gave some to her husband, who was with her, and he ate it. Then the eyes of both of them were opened, and they realized that they were naked; so they sewed fig leaves together and made loincloths for themselves. (Gn 3:1-7)

Adam and Eve had it all. They had a garden to live in, built by God himself. All they had to do was tend it. They had the help of all the animals. They had anything they wanted to eat. They had a perfect marriage, in which they were perfectly suited to each other, and plenty of interesting and useful work to do. They had an intimate relationship with God their Creator and could look forward to everlasting life. They only lacked sin, shame, strife, suffering, sickness, and death. The third chapter of Genesis explains how they threw it all away. They lost what they had—not just for themselves, but for the whole human race descended from them—and introduced sin into the world. With sin came all the problems that are its consequences.

The instigator of their trouble was the serpent, identified with Satan, the devil, the angelic being who first rebelled against God. He was not trying to do Adam and Eve a favor. Rather he was envious of their happiness: "By the envy of the devil, death entered the world" (Wis 2:24). But they had to consent to his plan. It was of their own free will that they abandoned what God had given them. Satan's plan of attack, whereby he convinced Eve to do the thing God had forbidden, was to undermine her faith.

His first ploy was to sow doubt and confusion. "Did God really tell you not to eat of any of the trees of the garden?" He is doing two things here. The first is to distort God's actual command from a prohibition of eating *one* tree's fruit to a prohibition of eating from *any* tree. The second is to introduce doubt: Did God *really* say that? These are methods he has not given up using. He still tempts people—you and me—to sin by using the same method today. "Is it *really* wrong to steal, to lie, to commit adultery? Did God really mean that as a commandment? Maybe it's just an ideal," he whispers in our ears.

Having weakened Eve's faith through doubt, he makes a frontal attack by simply denying what God has said. God had told them, "You will die"; Satan says, "You will not die." He follows this up by suggesting that God is keeping Eve from something good. "Your eyes will be opened and you will be like gods," he says, implying that God is not the bountiful and kind Father that Eve has known, but a cruel tyrant. Her faith in God's truth and in God's goodness are his target here. He hasn't given up on that lie either. "It's all right to help yourself to all the pleasure and wealth you can get. You need it. It's unfair to deny yourself that learning experience. That's how you'll find fulfillment." How many times have we heard that kind of thing rationalized?

Without faith in God, Eve disobeyed the command of God and easily induced her husband to do the same. He was the first person in the world to do something he knew was wrong "because everybody's doing it." The consequences have been enormous. Sin and death entered the world, and with them all the problems that afflict human life. Disobedience was the sin, but the first step in disobedience was to abandon faith in God's word and in his goodness.

The first sin began with a lack of faith; the solution to sin is the obedience of faith. This is the message of the gospel: that the evils of the world that began with doubt and denial can be overcome by faith.

Study: Genesis 3.

1. Read Genesis 2:15-25.
What command does God give to the man and the woman? What are the consequences of breaking it?

(a) _____

_____

(b) _____

_____

Describe the relationship of the man and the woman as depicted in this passage.

_____

_____

_____

_____

How does it compare with the average marriage in our modern-day society?

_____

_____

_____

2. Read Genesis 3:1-7.

What does the serpent tell the woman?

_____

_____

Find the commands and statements of God that Satan contradicts and Eve's response to Satan's temptations. Then fill out the chart below.

Command/Statement of God	Satan's Contradiction	Eve's Response

What are the first consequences of the man's and the woman's disobedience?

_____

_____

3. Read Genesis 3:8-19.

What has now changed in the man's and the woman's relationship to God?

_____

_____

_____

How do they explain their actions to God?

_____

_____

What consequences does God promise for the woman? For the man? How is their relationship to be changed?

(a) The woman: _____

_____

(b) The man: _____

_____

(c) Their relationship: _____

_____

To give you a better appreciation of what happened when sin and death entered the world, go back and re-read Genesis 2:15-25. Now imagine for just a couple of minutes what life would be like today without the fall. Identify three ways in which it would be different.

1. _____

_____

_____

2. _____

_____

3. _____

_____

Summary:

Read over your notes from this study and summarize them below. How have you experienced temptations similar to those described here? How can you see the consequences of sin described here in your own life and the lives of others? Mention two specific ways in which the fall has affected your own life.

1. Summary of study: _____

_____

_____

_____

_____

_____

2. One way: _____

_____

3. Second way: _____

_____

Tip for Growing in Faith:

The questions the serpent asked Eve are of course still very much around today. Satan still uses them to tempt us. But we can turn them against him to make faith an aid in overcoming temptations.

When soldiers are preparing to go into a situation where they may be taken prisoner and interrogated, they often take a special course in defeating the tricks used by interrogators to break their will and make them reveal secrets. Once they know the trick, they won't fall for it. We can do the same with our enemy, Satan.

Since we know these questions and where they lead, we can listen for them and be prepared to answer them in no uncertain terms. "Did God really say . . . ?"—if we study God's Word and the teaching of the church we can answer clearly, "Yes, he did!" When Satan promises us fulfillment and suggests that God's commandments are unfair, we should remember the love and goodness of God that we know by faith. Thus two of Satan's sharpest weapons can be blunted.

Optional Memory Verse:

For just as in Adam all die, so too in Christ shall all be brought to life.
(1 Cor 15:22)

For Group Discussion:

1. What were the consequences of the fall?

2. What tactics did the devil use in tempting Eve?

3. How did Eve respond to Satan's temptations? What should she have done?

4. What was the role of Adam in the fall? What should he have done?

5. Discuss the effects of the fall that you see in the world around you. How can you and those you love remain faithful to God in the world today?

Study 6—Romans 6:1-11
Faith Overcomes Sin

How can we who died to sin yet live in it? Or are you unaware that we who were baptized into Christ Jesus were baptized into his death? We were indeed buried with him through baptism into death, so that, just as Christ was raised from the dead by the glory of the Father, we too might live in newness of life.

For if we have grown into union with him through a death like his, we shall also be united with him in the resurrection. We know that our old self was crucified with him, so that our sinful body might be done away with, that we might no longer be in slavery to sin. (Rom 6:2-6)

What's the worst thing that could possibly happen to you? Sometimes, to express how bad a thing is, we call it a "fate worse than death." But really, death is the worst thing, the final closing off of all options. We sometimes say, "Where there's life, there's hope." No matter what happened, if you survived, you'd say, "Well, at least I'm still alive. Maybe I can make something of this situation." To desire one's own final extinction is not natural. What is natural is to fear death. Behind every other fear that we have lurks the fear of death.

So what if you knew that death was not the end after all? The "King of Terrors" would lose his ability to frighten, and with him all the other fears that plague our lives. What if death were not only not the end, but if it were in fact the gateway to a new and better life? We could look forward to escaping from the problems of this world, which are caused by sin, into a life without sin or sorrow. Wouldn't that be good news?

That is good news. In fact, that is the good news, the gospel. Because Jesus died and rose from the dead, death need no longer terrify. Death has been conquered, and with it the fear of death that holds us in bondage to sin. The plan that Satan began by the deception of Adam and Eve has been foiled. The disobedience of the first human beings brought death into the world; the obedience of Jesus Christ destroyed it. This good news has the power to set free those who hear and accept it, who make it a part of their lives.

This good news concerns something that is unseen. We see death all around us. We do not see eternal life. Therefore accepting the good news when we hear it is an act of faith. As Paul says of the gospel:

For I am not ashamed of the gospel: it is the power of God for salvation to every one who has faith, to the Jew first and also to the

Greek. For in it the righteousness of God is revealed through faith for faith; as it is written, "He who through faith is righteous shall live."
(Rom 1:16-17, RSV)

When Jesus sent out his disciples, he commanded them to proclaim this gospel. "Whoever believes and is baptized will be saved," he told them (Mk 16:16). Baptism, Peter explains in his first letter, "is not a removal of dirt from the body but an appeal to God for a clear conscience, through the resurrection of Jesus Christ" (1 Pt 3:21). Therefore Paul speaks to those who have accepted the gospel as "we who have been baptized into Christ." Baptism makes us participants in all that Christ has done, in dying and rising from the dead, so that we live as part of that unseen reality.

Paul could go so far as to say to the Galatians:

"I have been crucified with Christ; yet I live, no longer I, but Christ lives in me; insofar as I now live in the flesh, I live by faith in the Son of God." (Gal 2:19-20)

Or as he says to the Romans, "Can we who died to sin yet live in it?" Our being saved from sin and death is not something that happened once and then was over. It is the beginning of a new way of life, a life of faith, a life that can only endure by the constant decision to accept the reality of things unseen. This way of life is the very opposite of the doubt and denial that the serpent induced in Eve. Paul describes this as a new way of thinking about oneself: "You too must think of yourselves as [being] dead to sin and living for God in Christ Jesus" (Rom 6:11).

If you have faith in the gospel, then, the worst thing that can happen has already happened. You have already died. All that remains is to strengthen the life of faith that is the living out of the gospel. It means standing firm where Adam and Eve failed, like the heroes of faith who acted on unseen realities, because: "You have died, and your life is hidden with Christ in God" (Col 3:3). "You have died"—already! So what is there to worry about?

Study: Romans 6:1-11.

1. Read Romans 5:12-21.
Here Paul contrasts Adam, the one person who brought death into the world, with Christ, the one person who brought salvation. For each of the following characteristics of the fallen life, what does Paul give as a contrast? How does Christ embody the new life in each case? To complete the assignment, look up the additional Scripture passages below and then fill out the chart.

Scriptural Reference	Characteristic of Fall	Contrast by Paul	New Life in Christ
(Rom 5:16; 2 Cor 5:18-21)	Sin		
(Rom 5:16; Rom 8:1-13)	Condemnation		
(Rom 5:19; Phil 2:5-11)	Disobedience		
(Rom 5:21; 1 Cor 15: 20-22)	Death		

2. Read Romans 6:1-4.
Paul here stresses baptism as the way in which we enter into Christ's death and resurrection. Look at these other references to baptism in the Scripture. How does each of these develop the meaning of baptism in the life of Christ or the Christian?

(a) Luke 3:16:

_____

_____

_____

(b) John 1:29-34:

_____

_____

_____

(c) Luke 12:50:

_____

_____

_____

(d) Mark 10:38-39:

_____

_____

_____

(e) Acts 2:38:

_____

_____

_____

(f) Acts 11:15-17:

_____

_____

_____

_____

3. Read Romans 6:5-11.

Paul discusses the implications of our new life in Christ. There are several important conclusions that follow for us because of what Christ has done. Each of the following verses mentions one. In each case, what is it that Christ's death and resurrection means for us?

(a) Verse 5: _____

(b) Verse 6: _____

(c) Verse 8: _____

(d) Verse 11: _____

In light of these implications, take several minutes to renew your own baptismal vows. Compose a prayer to the Lord. Write it below.

_____

_____

_____

_____

_____

_____

_____

Summary:

Look over your notes from this study. The passages we have studied here are some of the most profound in all of Scripture. Consider them prayerfully. Consider especially what you might need to do in order to act on them. What are the implications of this Word of Scripture for your life?

_____

_____

_____

_____

_____

_____

_____

_____

Tip for Growing in Faith:

Living the life of faith means being dead to sin. It implies a break with a life lived in sin and without faith and an acceptance of the reality of Jesus Christ and his gospel. You have just renewed your baptismal vows. That is an important step in breaking with sin and living a life of faith. But there is something else that you can do to accept this reality in your life today.

If you have never consciously accepted the gospel of Jesus Christ, you can do it now. Repent of any lack of faith, any denial of the Lord, and of any wrongdoing you may have committed. Then offer your life to the Lord Jesus. Tell him that you believe he is the Savior, that he died and rose from the dead. Tell him you want to believe in him and belong to him from now on. Then the baptism you have just reaffirmed can begin to have an even greater impact on your life. Of course, if you have never been baptized, you should seek out a program of instruction that will lead to baptism.

If you have already made a conscious decision to give your life to God at some time in the past, you can still do it again. Offer your life once again to Christ as a living sacrifice. If in any way you have failed to live up to your profession of faith, repent and ask for God's forgiveness and salvation once again.

The life of faith is not "business as usual" but a constant turning to Christ and looking for his salvation. We are not a finished product until we finally enter heaven and behold God face to face!

Optional Memory Verse:

You too must think of yourselves as [being] dead to sin and living for God in Christ Jesus. (Rom 6:11)

For Group Discussion:

1. Why do you suppose almost everyone fears death? Discuss.

2. Why do we have good reason not to fear death as Christians?

3. How do we enter from death into new life in Christ? What exactly does this new life in Christ involve? Hint: Review your study sections on the Letter to the Romans, especially Romans 6:5-11.

4. What exactly do we do when we renew our baptismal vows? Have someone in the group read the church's prayer for the renewal of baptismal vows and then discuss what it means.

5. Review the "Tip for Growing in Faith." Discuss.

Part III:

Three Important Helps to Living a Life of Faith

In our last study, we saw how Jesus is the answer to our predicament. But our Christian life isn't over once we come to have faith in Jesus; it is just beginning. We need to nurture our life of faith in God. During our last three studies, we will explore three important ways God has given us to grow in faith: (1) prayer, (2) the holy Scriptures, and (3) the Eucharist.

Study 7—Matthew 6:5-15
Prayer Nurtures Our Relationship with God

"When you pray, do not be like the hypocrites, who love to stand and pray in the synagogues and on street corners so that others may see them. Amen, I say to you, they have received their reward. But when you pray, go to your inner room, close the door, and pray to your Father in secret. And your Father who sees in secret will repay you." (Mt 6:5-6)

Jesus expects those who believe in him and follow him to pray. You've probably heard prayer spoken of as a religious duty, perhaps often enough that you might take it for granted. Did you ever stop to ask why you should pray?

It might seem that if you really had faith, you would not pray. After all, if God exists and wants to do good things for you, then he already knows better than you what you need, so why ask for it? But in fact, prayer is a way of growing in faith.

The most important thing is not *how* you pray, but *that* you pray. Jesus doesn't say, "If you pray." Most of the time, he doesn't even tell people to pray. He just says, "When you pray," assuming prayer as a normal part of his followers' lives. He also encourages his followers to ask for things. "Ask and it will be given to you," he says in Matthew 7:7. Asking takes some faith: the faith that God exists and that he is willing to give what you ask for. But there is more to prayer than that, and this passage from Matthew 6 gives Jesus' clearest directions for prayer. It also shows us how prayer is a means of growing in faith.

Jesus begins by telling us not to pray like "the hypocrites," referring to certain Jews of his day who liked to perform religious duties in public. They are getting what they really want, he says: the approval of the other people around them. They pray to act pious, but that is not why we should pray. He goes on to contrast his followers with the pagans who "babble" because they "think that they will be heard because of their many words" (Mt 6:7). This does not mean that we should not be persistent in prayer. Elsewhere Jesus taught his disciples to "pray always without becoming weary" (Lk 18:1). He is referring to pagan techniques of repeating names and formulas in the hope that one magic formula will "do the trick" and force the god entreated to do something. Prayer is not a magic formula any more than it is a way of gaining praise for our great piety.

Instead, Jesus tells us to go and pray in an "inner room" with the door closed. Prayer is talking to God as our Father "who sees in secret" and who "knows what you need before you ask him" (Mt 6:8). Our reliance in prayer is not on public opinion or on techniques—both of which can be seen. Rather, it is on God, who is unseen. That is why prayer exercises our faith. When we pray in this way, we are doing something that does not make any sense unless something that we cannot see is real. Such prayer is a daily act of faith.

Furthermore, prayer as Jesus taught it is a way of entering more completely into the world of faith. After giving two ways not to pray, Jesus gives some direction on how to pray. The familiar Lord's Prayer that Jesus teaches here (Mt 6:9-13) has been the most basic Christian prayer ever since. Long books could be—and have been—written about it. Here I will point out only that it begins and ends by asking for things that relate to the life of faith, the life of God. "Hallowed be thy name; thy kingdom come, thy will be done"—these petitions focus on God, and if they are accomplished through us and in us, we must necessarily be more a part of God's life. At the end we pray, "Lead us not into temptation, but deliver us from evil." In these petitions we are asking to be removed further from the life of sin and death and more into the unseen life of God.

In the middle, this prayer highlights two things. First, we ask for our "daily bread." This stands for everything we need, and expresses our total dependence on God. We also ask to be forgiven as we forgive others. Jesus develops this point further in Matthew 6:14-15: "If you forgive others their transgressions, your heavenly Father will forgive you. But if you do not forgive others, neither will your Father forgive your transgressions." Jesus also makes forgiveness a condition of receiving what we ask for in Mark 11:25. Forgiveness is part of the life and character of God that we take on when we live the life of faith.

So praying, and especially praying the prayer that Jesus taught us, is essential to growing in faith. To pray is to allow the life of faith to take us over, so that we can say more and more truly, "The life I now live in the flesh I live by faith in the Son of God, who loved me and gave himself for me" (Gal 2:20, RSV).

Study: Matthew 6:5-15.

1. In the Old Testament, there are numerous examples of people who prayed. They did so on many occasions and for many different reasons. To get some idea of the many ways in which human beings can address God, look at the following biblical figures. In each case, fill out the chart below by giving the reason or occasion for the prayer and its purpose.

Scripture Passage	Reason or occasion	Purpose
Isaac (Gn 27:27-29)		
Moses (Ex 32:7-14)		
Solomon (1 Kgs 3:4-14)		
Elijah (1 Kgs 18:36-39)		
Hezekiah (Is 38:9-20)		
Daniel (Dn 9:3-19)		
Sarah (Tb 3:7-15)		

2. Read Matthew 6:1-18.
Here Jesus gives instruction about performing several different religious duties. For each of them, what does he say one is not to do? What is one to do? How is faith involved in each case? Supply your answers in the chart below.

Religious Duties	Not to Do	To Do	Faith Involved
Almsgiving (6:1-4)			
Prayer (6:5-8)			
Fasting (6:16-18)			

3. Read Matthew 6:9-13.
This is the great prayer that Jesus gave to his disciples, sometimes called the Lord's Prayer. Throughout the history of the church, it has been the most basic of all Christian prayers, the foundation of the prayer life of the church as a body and of individual Christians. Consider each of the parts of this prayer. Briefly note how they can become a prayer of faith for your life personally.

(a) "Our Father in heaven, _____
hallowed be your name,
your kingdom come, _____
your will be done,
on earth as in heaven." _____

_____

(b) "Give us today
our daily bread"; _____

_____

(c) "and forgive us our
debts, as we forgive
our debtors"; _____

_____

(d) "and do not subject
us to the final test,
but deliver us from
the evil one." _____

_____

Summary:

Look over your notes from this study. Consider what you have learned about prayer. How can you incorporate what Jesus says about prayer into your own life of faith? Mention two specific ways you can do this.

1. Summary of notes: _____

_____

_____

_____

_____

_____

2. Application #1: _____

_____

_____

3. Application #2: _____

_____

_____

Tip for Growing in Faith:

If you haven't developed the habit of daily personal prayer, the best tip for growing in faith through prayer is that you do it. I found that when I made the decision to take time each day for personal prayer, it revolutionized my life. With each passing year I have gained a deeper conviction of the reality of Jesus Christ.

Personal prayer is simply spending time before the Lord, pointing ourselves in his direction. Even if we do not feel inspired or do not experience anything, turning toward God lets him know that we want him. Even if we do not know what to say, we can simply sit and look at him.

One way to find something to say is to use the Book of Psalms from Scripture. These prayers are inspired by the Holy Spirit. Jesus prayed these prayers, and the prayer of the church throughout her history has been based on them. They are, in effect, God's revelation as to how he wants us to pray. If we use them, they can form our own prayers. Try simply reading one or two psalms aloud, reflecting on the words as you do so. If you do this regularly every day, you will find that you understand more and more about how to pray to God.

Optional Memory Verse:

"But when you pray, go to your inner room, close the door, and pray to your Father in secret. And your Father who sees in secret will repay you."
(Mt 6:6)

For Group Discussion:

1. What is the most important thing about prayer? Why?

2. How is prayer a means of growing in faith? Explain.

3. Jesus tells us not to make a public display of our prayer. Why?

4. In the Old Testament Scripture passages we reviewed for individual study, we saw important biblical figures praying on many different occasions and for many different reasons. What does this tell us about the role of prayer in living a life of faith? Discuss.

5. Let everyone in the group share one instance of growing in faith through personal prayer.

Study 8—Acts 17:11-12
God Reveals Himself to Us in Scripture

These Jews were more fair-minded than those in Thessalonica, for they received the word with all willingness and examined the scriptures daily to determine whether these things were so. Many of them became believers, as did not a few of the influential Greek women and men.

(Acts 17:11-12)

The Bible is not like any other book you have read. It is not merely beautiful sentiments, interesting stories, or useful facts. It is a book that expresses God's revealed word—truth beyond what any human being could conceive. The revelation contained in sacred Scripture is the unseen reality that is the object of our faith. It is what we accept and decide to believe because God has revealed it. Therefore reading Scripture is an important way to grow in faith.

That is what the Jews of Beroea described in this passage knew. Paul and Silas had just come to their city, proclaiming that Jesus was the Messiah, the one sent by God. When they heard the gospel, they received it "with all willingness," that is, they were prepared to accept it and to put their faith in it. Acting on this willingness, they "examined the scriptures"—that is, the Old Testament—"to determine whether these things were so." They were looking in the right place. The way to find out if anything is deserving of faith is to see how it accords with God's revelation. The result was that "many became believers." Faith, Paul tells us, "comes from what is heard" (Rom 10:17). So the increase and confirmation of faith came to the Beroean Jews by heeding the Word of sacred Scripture.

It can come to us today in the same way. The Jews of Paul's day had only the Old Testament. By the inspiration of the Holy Spirit, the apostolic church produced and accepted the canonical New Testament which forms the core of the church's deposit of faith. We have, in the full canon of Scripture that the church hands on to us and authoritatively interprets, an infallible guide to the things of faith.

But it is more than mere facts. It is something we can feed on spiritually. Through God's Word in Scripture we can allow our minds and hearts to be formed into the image of God's mind and heart. This is what Paul meant when he exhorted Timothy to study the Scriptures: "All scripture is inspired by God and is useful for teaching, for refutation, for correction, and for training in righteousness" (2 Tm 3:16). God's revelation carries with it the presence of God's Spirit who inspired it, so that reading the Scripture is like having God speaking to you in person. The reading of Scripture can have stunning effects on people.

In the second book of Kings (2 Kgs 22:8-13), we read of one such example. Josiah king of Judah had ordered extensive renovations to the Temple. In the course of the work, the workmen discovered a book containing the law of the Lord, probably a copy of the Book of Deuteronomy. When they read it to him, he realized that the people of Judah had not been following the law. He "tore his garments" as a sign of mourning and set about a major reform in the life of his kingdom. After the exile, when Ezra the scribe read the Book of the Law to the people, they fell down on their faces and began to weep because they realized their sins (Neh 8:1-12).

In the New Testament, too, we can see other examples of conversion as a result of reading the Scriptures. Acts 8:26-40 tells the story of an Ethiopian eunuch, a high official in that country, who had some acquaintance with Judaism. As he was reading the Scriptures in his chariot, he met Philip, who explained that the passage he was reading was in fact a prophecy about Jesus. The explanation of God's Word brought the eunuch to faith in the gospel at once.

In all these cases, reading, hearing, studying, and understanding the Word of God in Scripture brought about an encounter with the living God. For us today, reading Scripture with faith can make God more present to us, thus strengthening our faith. In reading the Scripture we must begin with some faith, that is, with the willingness to accept God's Word as true. We also need to see it as addressed to us personally. If we do, we will find that our faith will be strengthened by deeper insight into God's character.

Study: Acts 17:11-12.

1. Read Matthew 4:1-10.
This passage describes how Jesus used Scripture as a defense against the temptations of the devil. In the wilderness, the devil offered Jesus three temptations. To each Jesus replied with a word of Scripture. Look up each passage Jesus quotes. For each temptation, describe how Jesus' reply indicates faith in God.

(a) To turn stones into bread (Mt 4:3-4; Dt 8:3)

_____

_____

(b) To throw himself from the temple (Mt 4:5-7; Dt 6:16):

_____

_____

_____

(c) To obtain power by worshiping the devil (Mt 4:8-10; Dt 6:13-14):

_____

_____

_____

Following Jesus' example, how can you use Scripture effectively in your own life when you face temptation?

_____

_____

_____

_____

2. In the Book of Acts, there are many occasions when the apostles used Scripture to bring about faith. Look at each of these passages, and look up the Old Testament passage being quoted or alluded to (sometimes it's not an exact quotation). In each case, how does Scripture build up the faith of those who hear it?

(a) Acts 2:25-28 (Ps 16:8-11): _____

_____

_____

(b) Acts 4:25-26 (Ps 2:1-2): _____

_____

_____

_____

(c) Acts 8:32-33 (Is 53:7-8): _____

_____

_____

_____

(d) Acts 13:47-48 (Is 49:6): _____

_____

_____

_____

(e) Acts 15:15-19 (Am 9:11-12): _____

_____

_____

_____

What can you learn from the example of the apostles about the role Scripture should play in your own life of faith?

_____

_____

_____

_____

_____

3. Read 2 Timothy 3:14-17.
In verse 16, Paul states that Scripture is "useful for teaching, for refutation, for correction, and for training in righteousness." Scan the studies you've done in this guide. What Scripture passages have been particularly useful to you: for teaching about faith; for refutation of the lies and temptations of the devil; for correction of bad tendencies in yourself or others; and for training in righteousness, that is, in God's ways? Write them below so you can remember to use them in the future.

(a) Teaching: _____

_____

_____

(b) Refutation: _____

_____

_____

(c) Correction: _____

_____

_____

(d) Training in righteousness: _____

_____

_____

Think about two areas of temptation in your own life where you are particularly vulnerable to attack and where the Scripture passages in this study could prove helpful. Summarize the temptation below and then write the Scripture references next to it.

1. _____

_____

_____

_____

_____

2._____

_____

_____

_____

Summary:

Look over your notes from this study. What have you learned about using Scripture to grow in faith? What particular resolution can you make to let it help you more in the future?

1. Summary of what I've learned: _____

_____

_____

_____

2. My resolution: _____

_____

_____

Tip for Growing in Faith:

One important way that Scripture can help us grow in faith is by being a personal message from God to us individually. If we say, "Well, that's all very well in general, but where's the part about me?" we will miss the point.

One way to overcome this problem is to read the Scripture, perhaps aloud, substituting your name for any general expressions. This way God's commandments become commands *to me*; God's promises become promises *to me*. For example, Romans 8:31 reads, "What then shall we say to this? If God is for us, who can be against us?" You might read that, "If God is for me, who can be against me?"

Try it sometime. The effects can be staggering.

Optional Memory Verse:

All scripture is inspired by God and is useful for teaching, for refutation, for correction, and for training in righteousness. (2 Tm 3:16)

For Group Discussion:

1. What makes the Bible such a special book?

2. What do we mean when we say God speaks to us through his Word in Scripture? Discuss.

3. Why do you suppose Jesus used Scripture as a defense against the temptations of the devil? Have you ever used Scripture as a defense against temptation? How? When?

4. Let everyone look up and read one Scripture passage from the study section on the Book of Acts. It should be a passage that was inspiring as a faith builder. Give the person who selected the passage an opportunity to explain why it was inspiring.

5. Have someone in your group read Isaiah 43 aloud with the "Tip for Growing in Faith" in mind. Each person in the group should let God speak directly to him or her as the passage is read. Let group members share their thoughts on the reading after a quiet time of reflection.

Study 9—John 6:26-71
Our Intimate Relationship
with Christ in the Eucharist

Jesus said to them, "Amen, amen, I say to you, unless you eat the flesh of the Son of Man and drink his blood, you do not have life within you. Whoever eats my flesh and drinks my blood has eternal life, and I will raise him on the last day. For my flesh is true food, and my blood is true drink. Whoever eats my flesh and drinks my blood remains in me and I in him. Just as the living Father sent me and I have life because of the Father, so also the one who feeds on me will have life because of me."

(Jn 6:53-57)

"A personal relationship with God"—that's a phrase you may have heard before. It's what God desires each of us to have. But how can such a thing happen? How can the infinite God have a personal relationship with finite human beings?

In this study on faith, we have seen a few of the ways. First of all, we need to have faith in God. We need to believe the gospel, the good news of what he has done for us in Jesus Christ, and make that a part of our life. In prayer we speak to God. In Scripture we can read the revelation of his will. Sometimes we can experience God speaking to us by his Holy Spirit. But God is not satisfied with that. He has given us a supreme way to a personal relationship with him. We can actually eat the body and blood of Jesus Christ in the Eucharist. We can be physically united with him and with his death and resurrection.

When Jesus promised this gift his hearers were astonished. They found it impossible to believe. They "quarreled among themselves, saying, 'How can this man give us [his] flesh to eat?'" (Jn 6:52); even some of his disciples said, "This saying is hard; who can accept it?" (Jn 6:60). Jesus did not tone down his promise, however. He insisted on its literal truth. When he said, "He who eats my body and drinks my blood has eternal life," the Greek word translated "eat" literally means "chew" or "gnaw," and was used especially for the eating of raw, rather than cooked, food. The relationship he promised through his body and blood is real and intimate.

Jesus fulfilled his promise during the Passover feast, the Last Supper with his disciples. The meal was a sacrifice commemorating the deliverance from Egypt, a sacrifice that was about to be fulfilled by Jesus himself by his death and resurrection. During the meal, "he took bread, and when he had given thanks he broke it and gave it to them, saying, 'This is my body which is given for you. Do this in remembrance of me.' And likewise the cup after supper, saying, "This cup which is poured out for you is the new covenant in my blood'" (Lk 22:19-20 RSV).

The association of blood and the covenant recalls the covenant between God and the people of Israel, when Moses sprinkled blood on the people to confirm their dedication to God's law (Ex 24:8). Thus the Eucharist that Christ instituted on that occasion is a perpetual participation in his saving sacrifice, when he shed his blood as a victim to reconcile the human race to God. Do we really fathom what this means for us?

When we approach the Eucharist with faith, what we believe in becomes real in us. We truly come in contact with the very life and saving action of God. It is not a gift to be taken lightly. Paul recalls the institution of the Eucharist in the First Letter to the Corinthians. He adds a warning on the need for faith in the bodily presence of Christ: "For anyone who eats or drinks without discerning the body, eats and drinks judgment on himself" (1 Cor 11:29). In the Eucharist we encounter the presence of the most holy God, so we must approach the banquet table with faith.

But it is an encounter which he desires us to have. Jesus offers us the bread of life, his own body and blood, and promises, "Whoever comes to me will never hunger, and whoever believes in me will never thirst" (Jn 6:35). He calls us to a personal relationship with him, where our faith can be strengthened by intimate union with him. The Eucharist makes this encounter a reality in our earthly lives. It is the closest we will come in this life to the union we will experience at the end of the road that we are traveling.

Let us appreciate this great gift that God has given us, the very gift of himself.

Study: John 6:26-71.

1. Read verses 26-40.
Here Jesus promises a "bread from heaven" greater than the manna that the Israelites ate in the desert during the Exodus under Moses.

The account of the manna is found in Exodus chapter 16. Read this account. Why does God give the Israelites this food?

What is there about the situation of the Israelites that is similar to the situation of the people in John 6?

_____

_____

_____

_____

How is Jesus in John 6 trying to change the crowd's way of thinking? How do they need more faith?

(a) _____

_____

(b) _____

_____

The feeding with manna is also referred to in Deuteronomy 8:3. How does this view of the manna compare to what Jesus says about the bread from heaven?

_____

_____

_____

_____

If the Eucharist is bread come down from heaven for us, how should we approach the table of the Lord?

_____

_____

_____

_____

2. Read verses 41-59.
Here the Jews make two objections to what Jesus is saying. What are they?

(a) _____

(b) _____

In responding to them, what does Jesus assert about himself?

_____

_____

_____

_____

What promises does he make? List them and number them yourself.

_____

_____

_____

_____

Prayerfully imagine yourself at this scene. What questions do you want to ask? How will you respond to Jesus?

(a) Your questions: _____

_____

_____

(b) Your response to Jesus: _____

_____

_____

3. Read verses 60-71.
Two different groups of people respond to Jesus in different ways. Who are they?

(a) _____

(b) _____

What are their responses? Number them yourself below.

_____

_____

_____

_____

Jesus gives reasons for the different responses. In each case, what are they? Number your answers.

_____

_____

_____

_____

Again, prayerfully imagine yourself at this scene. How will you respond to Jesus?

_____

_____

_____

_____

_____

_____

Go back and reread John 6:26-71. Reflect on the fact that this same Jesus comes to you in the Eucharist every Sunday. Do you truly accept what he has to offer? Or do you treat him casually and then simply get on with your day? Write down your reflections.

_____

_____

_____

_____

_____

_____

_____

_____

Summary:

Read over your notes from this study. What have you learned about the Eucharist and its connection with faith? What one resolution can you make to grow more in faith in this area?

1. What I have learned: _____

_____

_____

_____

_____

2. My resolution: _____

_____

_____

_____

_____

Tip for Growing in Faith:

Too often, receiving the Eucharist can become routine. If we receive the Lord's Body and Blood without paying attention to what we are receiving, he is still very much present, but we will not be much built up in faith by the encounter.

If we were about to be introduced to some important figure on earth, like a president or a king, we would be very careful to prepare ourselves. We would want to be wearing our best clothes, and take care that they be clean. We would try to be as polite as possible. We would pay close attention to what the person said and did. In the Eucharist, we are being introduced to the most important person in the universe, the Lord Jesus Christ, the Son of the Living God.

This is why the great spiritual teachers of the Church have consistently demanded that we come to the Eucharist with clean hearts, repentant for our sins, and laying aside the concerns of our daily life. Our attitude, how we pay attention, even how we sit in church, will encourage the inner attitude of faith that will enable us to hear the Lord speak to us. After we have received his Body and Blood, we should spend some time in prayer, listening for what he says to our hearts, and then thanking him for the gift of himself that he has given to us. In this way, the Eucharist will be able to build our faith and bring us more and more into the unseen life of God.

Optional Memory Verse:

"Whoever eats my flesh and drinks my blood has eternal life, and I will raise him on the last day." (Jn 6:54)

For Group Discussion:

1. Why is the Eucharist such a special gift to us?

2. Why do you think Jesus chose the Last Supper to institute the Eucharist? What does this tell us about the Eucharist?

3. What should our frame of mind and attitude of heart be when we receive the Eucharist? Discuss.

4. Have someone read the "Tip for Growing in Faith" aloud to the rest of the group. Then discuss ways you can approach the Eucharist with greater reverence and attentiveness.

5. Give everyone a chance to share how the Eucharist has helped them grow in faith. For instance, some people have found daily Communion to be an important way of staying close to the Lord.